FOREWORD
by Dean Elder

Born in Barcelona in 1893. Federico Mompou studied piano with Pedro Serra at the Barcelona Conservatory until 1911. A recital by Gabriel Fauré and Marguérite Long during the 1909-10 season influenced him deeply and he decided then and there to become a composer, to go to Paris to study.

Mompou left for Paris in November 1911 with a letter of recommendation from Enrique Granados for Fauré, the director of the *Conservatoire*. But in the waiting room the shy young pianist became so frightened, he left without even talking to Fauré. Later Mompou studied piano with Louis Diémer and harmony and composition with Emile Pessard who was impressed with his student's natural talent but impatient with his shyness. "When Mompou told him he wanted to compose, Pessard said brusquely, *'Alors composez, composez!'* And that is exactly what Mompou started to do the next day."[1] In composing he followed his own instincts, reacting violently against the strict rules of musical theory. He spent from 1914 to 1920 in Barcelona in the Spanish military service, composing in secret. During these years he developed his artistic tenets and style.

In 1920 he returned to Paris, became acquainted with the works of Satie and Ravel, and continued his friendship with his teacher Ferdinand Motte-Lacroix who first performed his works and had some published. He also met the eminent French critic, Émile Vuillermoz and his Spanish compatriot, the famous pianist Ricardo Viñes. Mompou began to be known by Paris high society, and his works began to be performed.

From 1931 to 1937 Mompou was active in the high society social life of Paris and published nothing. He began to long for solitude, and during the Second World War he returned to Barcelona in 1941. There he still remains leading a solitary life, dedicated to composing. He apparently needed the isolation of Barcelona, rather than the high society of Paris, to dream and experience his musical sensations.

Mompou has come to the United States three times to perform his works, his most recent visit being March 1978 for a concert with Alicia DeLarrocha and José Carreras in celebration of his 85th birthday. He speaks of his craftsmanship: "I have always tried to create perfect works, where all the measures are of the same quality. I'm convinced that the form I carry within me is like a power or destiny I can't get rid of and that simultaneously results in being the power of my music and one of its maxims. I used to work at the piano. But lately I try singing or imagining the developing of a melodic line...I can develop a theme without thinking much about it...It seems as if my music were my hands, hands which try at the keyboard until they get the group of keys to be depressed. Sometimes this trying leads me to the musical flow."[2]

Mompou's music is introspective, personal, sensuous, sometimes song-like, sometimes dance-like, with a popular folk quality. Often tinged with sadness, the music is dreamy and impressionistic, but always melodic and colorful — exquisite miniatures.

For students Mompou is a delightful discovery, and for concert artists he is a beloved friend.

♪ Notes on
"Songs and Dances Nos. 5, 6, 7, 8"

The melodies in *Songs and Dances Nos. 5 and 6* are original. *No. 5* (1942), one of Alicia DeLarrocha's favorites, is religious and Castilian in mood. The *lento liturgico* in C♯ melodic minor is of great beauty, dignity, and depth. The E major Dance, reminiscent of Paganini's *Caprice* in E major, is somewhat difficult because of the subtly-changing left hand broken-chord accompaniment. A *semplice-cerimonioso* trio in A major interrupts the Dance.

Song and Dance No. 6 (1943), harmonized with right-hand consecutive thirds, was one of Gina Bachauer's favorites and is dedicated to Artur Rubinstein. The languid Song sounds the sad complaint of the *criolla nostalgia* and the Dance's rhumba cross-rhythm measures are delightful.

Song and Dance No. 7 (1945) in A major returns to popular motives: the Song is *"Muntanyes regalades"* and the Dance is *"L'Hereu Riera."* If you do not own another note of Mompou, you should own this Song. It is of such subtle melodic intensity, harmonic and inner voice coloring and builds so strongly, that when played in an intimate atmosphere it can bring tears. Each phrase is perfectly constructed, building emotionally with each added color. Mompou masterfully adds enriching seconds and sixths to chords to make the vibrations more beautiful. There is never one note too many or too few.

Song and Dance No. 8 is also moving. Both the Song (*"Testament d'Amelia"*) and the Dance build to *forte* sonorities with *stretto* imitations in the inner or bass voices.

1. "Federico Mompou" by Santiago Kastner, Madrid; Consejo Superior de Investigaciones. Cientificas, 1947, translated by Dean Elder.
2. Ibid.

Adapted from *Clavier* (December 1978, pp. 14-20), © *The Instrumentalist Company* 1978. Used by permission of *The Instrumentalist Company*.

*The sketch of chapel and cypresses by Mompou
is found on all his compostions.

CANCIÓN Y DANZA 5

(Song and Dance No. 5)

FEDERICO MOMPOU

DANZA
(senza rigore)

A·Arthur Rubinstein

CANCIÓN Y DANZA 6
(Song and Dance No. 6)

FEDERICO MOMPOU

DANZA
Ritmado, ♩.= 144

CANCIÓN Y DANZA 7
(Song and Dance No. 7)

FEDERICO MOMPOU

CANCIÓN Y DANZA 8
(Song and Dance No.8)

FEDERICO MOMPOU

Moderato cantabile con sentimento

più sonoro ma no forte

DANZA (♩ = 160)